by Wanda Coleman

Mad Dog Black Lady (1979)
Imagoes (1983)

WANDA COLEMAN

IMAGOES

Black Sparrow Press

Santa Barbara - 1983

ACKNOWLEDGEMENT

Grateful acknowledgement is made to the editors of the following magazines where some of these poems have previously appeared: *Alcatraz 1 & 2, Bachy, California State Poetry Quarterly, Contact/II, Contemporary Quarterly of Poetry and Art, Day Tonight/Night Today, Electrum, Hawaii Review, L.A. Weekly, Los Angeles Times, Obras, Ouija Madness, Partisan Review, Post-Modern Writing, Sing Heavenly Muse!, Southbay Magazine, Stance, Sunset Palms Motel, Third Eye, 13th Moon, Washington Review, The Westerly Review,* and *Zephyr*.

LIBRARY OF CONGRESS CATALOGING IN PUBLICATION DATA

Coleman, Wanda.
  Imagoes.

  I. Title.
PS3553.04744I4   1983   811'.54   83-11949
ISBN 0-87685-510-9
ISBN 0-87685-509-5 (pbk.)
ISBN 0-87685-511-7 (lim. ed.)

for Lewana Mae Scott and George Evans

TABLE OF CONTENTS

1

2

IMAGOES

1

labor in this city flesh
neon womb/mother cement

IN SEARCH OF THE MYTHOLOGY OF DO WAH WAH

the melodrama continues
we personifications of classic greek-roman tragedy/history
play a continuous bill
nightly show in hell/hades featuring spades of every
    co-mingling/variation:
sound trumph of defeat as the laboring armies of egypt retreat
before the thundering chariots of corporate roma
and medea, fleeced by her common law husband
loads the saturday night special—turns it on her children
then herself—free at last from poverty's grasp
meanwhile echo overdoses on seconal
while pimp narcissus cruises avenues in search
of fresh meat and bigger mirrors
how many falls from success's skyscraper must icarus take
before he learns that all the wax and feathers of a high school
    mis-education
will net him is a spot on the sidewalk
pandora's box is a festering place for venereal disease, tricks
and a boon to abortion clinics
and apollo's sun was permanently eclipsed by the television
    network
hatchet boys who are "tired of that niggah's antics"
mourning does indeed become electra whose brother's heroin habit
    was
paid for by ripping off their parent's home and sistuh antigone
pickets creon the police commissioner vainly charging brutal
    tactics
against her brothers and sisters of skin and economic plight while
oedipus, spawned on the breeding plantations of civil war america
slays his white father and covets his black mother
and sisyphus, worshipper of blue-eyed jesus perpetually
rolls his burdensome boulder of faith up the precipice of white
    humanity

while vulcan—in the sweltering pit of his ghetto discovers
department stores are flammable
alas ulysses set sail/revolutionary ex-patriot journeying round the
    world
to escape oppression returns years later
to declare "america ain't so bad after all" and
black orpheus the painter/poet/musician/dreamer
turns back to find fame and immortality a vanished eurydice
as our caesars die prematurely
under the daggers of suspicious, envious, traitorous toms
lead by a sincere but deluded brutus

        the fault dear fellow blacks
        is not in our astrology charts
        but in our society
        that we are run under

DADDYBOY

1

with papa walking toward sunset
along the old railroad tracks in watts off 103rd
i am five in braids and bangs
and the blue cornflower print jumper mama made
the sun, a big copper smile
peeks over thunderheads
papa holds my tiny brown hand in his huge
boxer's fist. we wave at the switchman as we
walk past. i skip to keep in his giant's step
kicking granite pebbles as i go
watching them skitter in our path
home to mama

2

me & brother george have been up to mischief
we think we can outrun daddyboy
and break for the front door. he runs us round
the house twice then passes us, laughing
we uh-oh surprise, stop in our tracks
and run back the other way
he spins round, catches us, holds me
in the visc of his calves as he
plucks george high into the air
and takes the tar out us

3

daddyboy surprises mommygirl
with fats domino's latest hit, *honey chile*
they go into a clinch/kiss and we start to sniggle
they put it on the victrola and

show us how to boogie woogie and lindy hop
we ooh ahh as he flips her over his back
and swings her between his legs
then they put on something slow
and send us off to bed

4

"daddyboy daddyboy daddyboy's home!"
we run to greet him
"don't call me that no more!" his bass
is sharp and harsh. we run crying to mommygirl
"your father's black. white people
disrespect black men by calling them boy
call him anything but"

5

we've been fighting. mom's gonna tell pop
our rear ends ache in anticipation
another whipping. mom uses a peach tree limb
all pop needs is those big powerful black hands
home, he lectures us. brother and sister
should love and respect. at 10 & 12
we're too big for such nonsense

george gets his first
i figure a way to save my butt. i stuff my britches
with a book wrapped in a towel like i saw on tv
george is hot tears and snot. it's my turn
WHOP WHOP WHOP. i fake a boo hoo
"what's this?" surprised he reaches in, pulls out
the towel. the book thuds to the floor
he laughs and laughs so hard
he's almost crying and spanks me at the same time
and i'm laughing and crying and we're
laughing together
and shit does it hurt

6

one terrible morning pop came home in a sweat
he'd gone to the shop as usual
everything was gone. the printing presses
the desks. the files. the ledgers. every damn thing
his partner had ripped him off

"what we gonna do?" mom wailed
"i don't know" he said real quiet
i went hot and cold
he paced the room, slammed open the door
and went back to the streets

it is the only time i've ever seen him cry
and they was killin' tears

7

the phone screams. i jump up from my sleep
it's mama. can i come? papa's fallen
against the bathroom door. she can't get it open
she doesn't know if he's hurt
it's the seizures again brought on by scar tissue
from where they removed the tumor. yes
i'm on my way. and as i'm about to leave
the phone rings again. no
i don't have to come. the boys are coming
she says

but i go anyway

8

i take my father to the hills of zion
for wednesday night prayer meet
i'm long since a woman

he's long since grayed and grandfather
he goes into his wallet for the card and gives
it to me, his hands swollen/cushionoid with
illness. perhaps i'd like to come some time?
when i'm not too busy? they have a good choir.
i take the card, say okay say maybe
and wait patiently as he struggles
to get out of the car with the aid of his cane
and makes his way toward the light
of the open door

AT THE RECORD HOP

bobby-soxers exchange clandestine feels
in dark hallways of junior high gym
young black bodies humped hard to
hully gully shimmy peanut butter

puberty

embarrassment
menstrual red stains white pleated skirt
catching on to 2-tone socks
when nylons are in
losing worn elastic in cotton panties
threatening to drop
a cherry bomb
into the eyes of hungry young men

the only girl not asked to dance

allegiance is pledged earnest honk honk
of low rider bird horn and street racers rule turf
with hot rubber and zip guns
me/the intellectual square looks on in maimed silence
wish

lonely bus ride home
up front staring straight ahead

in the back of the bus
giggles. eager hands. lips learn to french

wonder why boys don't like me

JERRY 1964

until her

he was trouble-shooting throughout the south
in the name of civil rights
and the student non-violent coordinating committee

there were midnight rides in the back woods
of mississippi, careening down muddy roads
chased by the klan in sheets & shotguns

there were boycotts, sit-ins, marches, freedom rides
and hootenannies/campfires where voices sang "we shall overcome"
the interracial holding of hands
while wine was passed and more folk songs sung
lots of hot southern nights
baptised between musky black thighs

there was little rock, fayetteville, jackson, macon
tallahassee, birmingham and tuscaloosa
confrontations with authority, the press
the white power structure and uncle tom

speeches and walks through the same rooms
inhabited by martin luther and coretta king
going to their church and baby sitting their children
basking in their greatness

hunger strikes. one lasted as long as 40 days and
40 nights/peace and hope flooding hearts of young america
the mixed couple nursing him back to health
on milk and honey

there were bomb threats/beatings/cattle prods
the dogs/THE SHERIFF/cess pools that passed for jails
the nightmare of women and children broke open
by billy clubs bleeding without medical attention
on bare stone floors

there were moments just missed by bullets
vomiting up fear crouched to the floor
the empty noose strung up on the porch/the cross torched
uttering prayers to god/any god
until the curses died down, the cars screeched off
and the harangue stopped

there was talk and more talk/camaraderie
and marijuana, his heart an open sore
weeping compassion for his fellow man

and more. adventure. glory. promise

till he went west to california, fell between
virgin cocoa thighs
till roots were planted/a child
rent to pay/day-to-day routine/a job to keep
a future to plan for

until her pussy got good he was happy

JERRY 1966

the husband is radical revolutionary red neck
a georgia cracker

the wife, he doesn't know her anymore
militancy, a seed takes root

his hunger ignites her own

in some states their union still illegal
black-to-white/mongrelization

there was the night the cops busted in
while they were fucking
(ideas as contraband/hoodoo)
it was the wrong apartment

the time watts burned
riots. sniper fire. tanks
national guardsmen in helmets & jungle zoots
he hid. they were making
all the whites leave. even the light-skinned
blacks had a hard time

she wondered how he made it thru the freedom rides
eyes accuse. fingers point
everywhere they go people gawk
she withdraws, sullen silent
he becomes adept at passing for black

she tries to love him
guilty, he cannot love himself

JERRY 1967

four hundred years of pressure

anxious eyes
who was his father? where was his place?

so what if he's white
so what if she's black

non-violent answer to his dream/guitar
strapped to back/her eyes find
their way into his song: miscegenation

in the restaurant at breakfast
the drunk dashiki called him honky
how dare she allow
whitey to befoul her womb

or the time outside the liquor store
the nigger junky picked his pocket
all they had in the world
seven dollars
he could not fight back

history lay between them
her hunger an ocean he could not swim

love did not survive injustice

opaque eyes. she couldn't protect him
nor he, she

FIRST AFFAIR

by the very nature of the fact that she was
young and inexperienced

(he reached into her panties. into wet)

and by virtue of his age and deep soft voice which
countered the ugly hard life etched into his umber mask

(seductor to seductee)

by virtue of her need for sex which was separate from
but did not preclude "true love"

(a husband bad backed and lacking)

the undress of her hunger his gentle touch
flesh to flesh such ancient loving hands

(he reached for her nipples. they rose)

he, a player on women could sex her
in moist warm cup of her ear empty his jazz
tongue/his passion to her clit

(thru the cracked door he watched their joining)

by virtue of his manhood/a husband's need
to prove himself her supreme lover

he accepted the arrangement

BROKE UP

not that the moment was without pain
she could not reconcile the
knifing/betrayal/by love of no love return

it did not matter that his flesh was shared
it could've gone on and on
as long as he had time for her/by love of love enrapt

she searched for ways to control jealousy
a solution to self doubt/debasement
a way to secure/love love

he took exit
and could not be reached by phone

the clock a deadly companion

it did not matter that sex was shared
it could've gone round and round
as long as he dicked her/love's trap

stupid

she gave up looking for a reason
turned on the gas

died. quiet

BURGLARS

they steal the dreams of old women and children
break & enter kind hearts
tear down bloody crucifixes and wall plaques praising god
early morning sod from their shoes
tracked across livingroom rugs

missing: a night of pleasure in his arms
            praise of eager ears
            bitter sting of auto exhaust

they take the things we've forgotten we need
ransack the closets of our memories
turn upside down the order of christian lies

stolen: a kiss and touch of his thigh
          childhood's country boogie man
          footsteps pausing at my door to knock

yes. there are sneak thieves, pick pockets & purse snatchers
a veritable crime wave in the heat/heart/hearth of city
they creep & crawl thru streets & alleys/our perceptions

they are never caught

MAMA'S MAN

whisper night wizard
whisper blood silence
whisper heroin notes/death's legend
life in the substrata:

> he's there, hat cocked jaunty angle
> a gangster who takes crime passionately
> men going to the moon mean nothing
> just money, pussy and smoke
> evilness has carved its mark across
> his skull—the signature of a bottle
> he can't tell the difference between
> cheap perfume or the genuine article
> no matter how adept the chemist
> his bitch arrives and takes her place
> a maze of eyelashes smooth brown thigh
> deep cleavage pearl tongue and synthetic
> platinum wig flashing earring silver
> satin desire
> he yawns, inspects her purse

wind tight wizard
artful scene drawn in dingy yellow
blow down the wrong tube
tell it like it is:

> locked in sweet hate's embrace
> strokes home a rhythm and blues single
> digs into wide thighs, pounds home
> she bucks face twisted in sex agony
> grunts, reaches, tries to stretch cause
> he's oooh soo long and uhhh the orgasmic
> light switch on. she catches in a convulsion
> slack/he moves quick. turns her
> enters from the rear, eases in the head

29

then deep down to the bone
when pain fades she bucks again and it's
hi ho silver satin cloud's passion
laughing as sunday morning dawns

tall dark on dark wizard
shakes 2 and splits
leaves hearts open bleeding
seed crowding ghetto schools
a couple of suicides and alcoholics
broads always weak for dick
he sticks it to 'em every time

ANTICIPATING MURDER

1

here are the streets
real as real as real
ugly
do you see motherfucker
do you see the ripe con
do you see the zombies in the field
they're after you
it took 20 years for that nightmare to come true
adventuress
adventuress

        bitch, get it thru your head
        batman is a cartoon and
        you cannot fly

i could run home to mama
no answer
too proud to ask for money again
owe enough already

high noon of my life
i go to meet my ex-lover on the killing floor
can't feel noble about it
can't feel anything

wait
waiting

when you come, my man
be sure you get me good
or i'll get you

do me good
so do us both a favor

2

shallow eye
hides murder
gentlemanly thing to do

wondering will it be quick
am i to be tortured?

disfigurement
throwing lye an old nigger trick
shallow eye
hides murder

> paul said, "watch people. watch their eyes
> you can't tell a person by their eyes
> people lie with their eyes. you have to
> watch 'em. watch 'em close, babe"

no protection
me? a killer too?
western surplus carries 22s
an ambush on a compton street corner
me in holster and chaps blowing smoke from the barrel

how low does low go?

shallow eye
romance shattered
his cold dick
pimping from his cold dick
failure and prostitution (dead man for a lover)
black and cobalt blue

wondering
will it come quick
i prefer death to disfigurement
life tough enough as is

reflection down gun barrel
hope it's clean/small mercy

glad when this be over

3

tremble

words come trembling out
scared of the future
doors of opportunity close
catch my foot

cold here in dark womb damp
wet matches
light switch broke
tremble

can't get warm enough
can't get cash enough
can't get love enough
can't get high enough

scared

opportunity kicks my ass
bare butt
sucking a pacifier
26 yr old infant on a know-it-all streak
growing up under the gun can kill you

but better than not growing up at all
being this old learning frightens

tremble
black hand against the sink
see wrists/see razor blade
think red rushing into mirror/eyes
smell gas and bodies
jews had auschwitz
you have america
tremble

next on the ticket?
slow dream of drain-energy
aspirin coma
dark womb's dampness

wet matches
blank stare into skin's night

don't know what in the fuck to do

4

sniper bullet
my name on it
under contract terms of
agreement betrayals run rampant. this time
my head on the platter

our last night together he said if he was
going to go (hold court in the street) he might as
well take memories. going down i vomited into his groin
to the last moment something inside rejected him
he couldn't ejaculate. when we stopped i was relieved

click of phone
he calls to haunt me
now i have a real ghost, a flesh and blood spook
who sports a mustache, beard and lives on corners
we used to be partners but mutual hate broke up the relationship

he wants to pursue me
i won't run
i sit here. wait
if it's direct confrontation
odds are 50-50
if i go down it will be fighting
if he ambushes me or sets me up for a
gangbanger then i'm sunk unless chance
does me a turn

gritting my teeth i watch days pass
cause there's nothing else
doing
no cries for help now
hit the streets try to catch a buck or two
some light-weight job until
luck comes by for another lay
in the meantime, i hope he knows what he's doing
that sniper of mine

goddamn i love him

wonder if he realizes how lonely life is
without enemies

APRIL IN HOLLYWOOD

cool brisk fingers in my hair
the fresh sweet bite of crisp red delicious apples
service stations with "sorry no gas" signs
palm trees. the american flag full mast and shouting
sun. the body shop in red black and white. wind
the black man in blue who's got to get to cerritos
on 55¢. latins stealing swigs of tequila from
a torn brown paper bag in the back of a bus
radios barking disco
dogs mute in the face of poverty
old white ladies with shopping bags as wrinkled
as their necks, in tattered wigs, black high-fashion
eyelashes and green mascara
crisp starched sagebrush narcs crawling campuses
for children dealing illegal drugs
sweaty gay runners in tennis shoes jogging up sunset
chinese japanese thai korean vietnamese and
soul food kitchen smells
the mindless roar of
traffic on the boulevards at rush hour
endless grey curbs of home

DINNER WITH A FRIEND

she has me over alone
it's crab stolen by her ex-lover the transsexual
and a zucchini & onion & cheese stew with white wine
it's delicious and we fence a little
as she tells me how much
she really wants to be my friend
and i've been thinking it over. i like the bitch
she has balls
and then she proceeds to tell me
how my husband came by a few days ago
to put the make on her

ON GREEN MONEY STREET

unable to buy things
he moves away
sheets cold white still avenues
i wait, anxious beneath the solitary lamp
listen for the echo of his steps

he never shows

at sunrise
i move on with the traffic

NIGHT OWL

i come out in dark black as black
relax the clutch/defense
be self/recharged
queen of zeon crowned in helicopter searchlight
(the party waits)
timid souls of day shed masks on command
new things conceived
old things released

truth is dark
dark is truth

ON SPEED

i hit the 10, Santa Monica's freeway east
the radio screams
i keep to the left lane, accelerate
monitoring the rear view for the highway patrol
my heart the base count w/a melody of *him*
love come to an end, unspent rage/violence
i want to kill him. want to fuck him. i want peace
i hit the 101, Hollywood's freeway north
cruise taking in the lights of L.A. overhead
the giant tit of 3/4 moon suckled by sky
and stars. october stars. the radio moans
i hit the underpass, merge w/traffic
on on on
the 405, San Diego's freeway south
circle sharp, down to the right then up over
the rise his eyes Moraga, Sunset beyond the hills
and on on on
the junction of the 405 to the 10 east again
on Santa Monica's freeway to the 101, Hollywood ahead
the radio shrieks

i am made of steel
and have 4 wheel drive

love is 85 miles per hour

PIGGING OUT

—for Austin

at the restaurant we sit down to wine
we are *so hungry*
the crisp appetizers/early loves
and lightly seasoned salad
we've developed appetites for the garlic & onion of life
gorging on a main course of dissatisfaction
over frustrated creativity sautéed in
economic plight
he chews over his brooklyn childhood
i pick at the tedium of youthful watts summers

we eat away the lousy jobs stunting our talent
we eat away the hot smog-filled day
we eat away the war in the headlines
we eat away the threat of nuclear holocaust
we eat away love-threatening pressures
we eat away the human pain we see/feel/
are stymied by

(pride is such thin dessert)

we eat until our smiles return
until fat and happy

PARKED

loud. funk blast thru walls
i feel it clear across the street
in the car, kicked back
surreptitious sips of sweet rosé from a paper cup
cools, cuts the smog
conjures up visions: our last time in bed
                              him pounding into me/base count

neighborhood of colors
black brown red orange beige & gold faces
beat down places conceal unexpected treasure
unmeasurable orgasm of tongue to
greasy red sauced ribs texarkana style

i wait 3 hrs for him to reappear
from the house where rhythm & blues scream
his score of cocaine and marijuana
hidden in his jock

                    our last moment together
                    on a street corner at midnight

i watch young thin black dreams
skate by on their way to the pool hall
to hustle errands for dimes & quarters

satisfied

not knowing the story
or how it ends

DIAGNOSIS: FUCK CONGESTION IN UPPER WOMB TRACHEA
WITH COMPLICATIONS

stone reflections
moon in my mouth
i choke on love bones

men come and go
phases of moon: seasons of bitter cool spring earth
                 sweat hot summer wind
                 frost red autumn sky
                 blood purple winter night

black men/oceanic waves wash over my body
the saltiness makes me itch
turn to tub, soap in hand to wash

men come and go
ring the doorbell, stay till dawn
to disappear suddenly
i wonder—was it a dream?
was i sharing my bed or have my nightmares
taken new directions

men come and go
i whisper to my shadow, "there's a qualitative
difference between a love and a fuck"

my body moves through window pane
glass shatters everywhere but
never touches me. crunch crunch
under my stone feet. it feels good *to smash*

my hands, strong around the throat
of my lover could so easily mangle

my vagina castrate like scissors—snip snip
blood sacrifice
i carry to the altar—burn his flesh
in worship of myself

my heart, granite against his chest
he speaks to me of love. it hits
against me and breaks—snap snap
the pieces lay like so many broken children
it doesn't frighten
the odor of death rising from my womb

men come and go
leave moist trails/unctuous trails of slugs
along my empty thighs

morning. i look at my ghosts—all i have
to remind me i'm real
not a figment
of someone's imagination

i turn to tub
soap in hand
step into warm water
lower myself into suds
wash away traces
of having been touched
my body, clean
glistens—a polished stone
moves through mirrors
stone reflections
sun in my mouth

i am choking

BLUE

night. i wait for him to come out of shadow

blue bruise my thigh i won the fight—that time
fell against the table into bed screaming
till he got hard and gentle as the blues
picked me up a broke toy

my favorite color

blue bruise my thigh after fight
pushed into blue mattress his hands at my throat/blue
choked. against my skin his balls blue ache to unload into me
blue nothing in my heart for him

blue day he came got his clothes left the key
blue funk deep blue violet mad my hands lost
what to do. a new life so sudden blue i miss him
eyes cobalt blue ache to explode. into me. an ending

purple california death at dawn blue

blue monday street rife with hustle muscle and winos
sipping blue grape mad dog 20/20

the color of outer space

THE CALIFORNIA CRACK

she didn't know he was so shook

it started in his system/an erratic prance
some mechanism gone wet
codeine induced cellulitis, acid trails and flashes

he had nightmares about his mother pinching him in his sleep
his youth authority internment
the scar up his ass where they removed some thing
the lesbian he loved in Yucaipa
the black bird smashed against the window
of the stolen car

he began to sweat out his nights
when he woke his long dark brown hair was plastered
to his head. he was always dripping

it got so she couldn't stand laying next to him
the stench nauseated her, caused her to vomit
sometimes she made him sleep outside on the porch
so she could get an occasional night's rest
but most times she took breath by mouth

he went to the hospital
they took tests and found nothing
he went to the police
profuse sweating was not a crime
he took daily showers
the water bill went up
the seams in his clothes began
to mold and erode
the sheets and comforter would not
wash clean

his septic sweat permeated everything
seeped down through the mattress into
the earth beneath their bed

one summer's midnight as they slept in his dampness
there was an earthquake
it measured 8.2 on the Richter scale
the bed split open the soft moist mouth of a scream
and she watched with mixed emotions
as he fell through

yes
there must have been
another life
i died
this is hell
and i have come here

it's all so fictitious

mfs won't leave me alone the mf i want is sick

fire at midnight: a black sun

saint joan of bone

splatt
another shadow on the sidewalk

(she's five minutes away on mars
he shoots the spoon)

why? it is the price all pay to be

one tongue   cosmic orgy of
one skin   *mind/flesh*
one world   spirit

free of babel

                              in the mirrored tray/his eyes
                              i find my nose
                              open for the snort/love you go
                                        down so sweet

married, filing separate return

how will i write you?
off like a bad check?
my pen bleeds love songs & lone nights
listens to the stereo's intermittent sigh
yes you love me yes i love you
yes the world has ended

mahn. de only animal what cry

RECORDER

names. still quiet mouths
the dead sing hope pain/the body

warmth

i work among them
my hands swift, move. much to be done
countless numbers of them ahead

looking back and looking forward
smile to myself

girl, you know, don't you

they paid out of their estates
billed for stilled breath
heritage of dust

filed under "T"

today i work among the dead
sort them out, set them straight
arrange them in neat piles

these silent numbers stare at me
across the manila distance

the hands of a cold absorbed god

MANUELA COME OUT THE KITCHEN

what good does it do begging crumbs
i begged a good long while
and have nothing
and shame! here you are competing with me
for nothing. shame
gal, get out the kitchen

yes, perhaps your opportunities are better
father mexico mines the earth for oil and
someday will have wealth and power

my father dies under the yoke/lash/noosc/bullet/unemployment
and misery in general. leaves me a bitter legacy of
rage hope dignity

manuela why must we be enemies?
is there not cake enough for us both
in this oven of wealth/America
and what of Kwang Cheng
and of Marguerita who's black as me? espanol
rolls from her tongue sweet as sangria
yes. your skin is lighter. that's no guarantee

manuela you be stubborn. be the fool
learn as i've learned

the cook gives away nothing
without taking it from your butt in blood

so what to do? you ask
join me. i'm dynamite in an apron
we'll kill the cook, take the recipe book
and make cake

enough for all

PRETTY FACE

keep a move on
she won't take you to the place of your design
and furthermore she don't have time
sexy eyes healthy thighs cocoa skin
and girlish breasts can't justify
pain unrevealed/bitter/negative
conditions summed up in lips
ever on verge of put down
would sooner slay
no need to stop and chat
leave her where she's at
don't intrude
she's hell to get into
hard life, bad attitude

ANGEL BABY

morning. she's an ugly bitch
map of last night's lust grey in grey dawn
tracks/lover's dried cum at her lips
along her neck and breasts litter of tourists
eager freak seers down star-lined
boulevards/her mystique
click cameras courting the rich/famous/profane

abandoned by her hasty cockhound
moist and sticky between billboards
mocks fame & fortune. she runs an
ambivalent tongue across
plaque caked gums and teeth, tastes
bitter residue/zeon & cocaine high

glitter her eyelashes pepper pillows
hollywood's hills as she struggles
to focus in on day, head throbs
blue and white and pink collar traffic headed
downtown—feels like she's been gangbanged
by a dozen record execs   hit single in her ears

in bad need of a face-lift, gal—years
catching up. she grunts, stretches
rises shakes and scratches her tangled smog-filled
crown and stumbles toward the jane

queen of the jet set no matter how many
lovers leave her for new york

PAM

called me long distance at midnight
woke me and told me
her father died in the hospital that evening
died while talking with her stepmom
in mid-laugh

she cried a bit
on her way to being bombed/a little booze
to lose the blues and memory, shares

that birthday party
the time i read the poems with the 4 letter words
and how her blind raven haired diabetic
dad of french and latin descent
liked me a lot less

tonight it is this recollection
transmitting warmth north
along the hot thin wires of hurt

i hear her smile and the slight slur says
she'll be okay in the good morning

ROSE

she's dead down there
he said, laughed and turned up the volume

i went out this afternoon
mail in her box. it's been four days

times i come and go. her window
owlish yellow eyes peer out nosy/hungry
i feel them. look to see
her hand disappear
the curtain falls back into place

times she runs after me. tattles
my son's bad mouth
my husband's bad attitude
the landlady's bad management

times she corrals me. a cup of coffee
a tour of her grandchildren
she speaks french spanish yiddish
an old egyptian jew. her man long dead
she never found another

times her hand full of palsy and edema
i write letters for her
type up her list of medications

times i watch her totter
down the block to the health spa
to release from arthritic pain

times the worst times
my feet my head my heart ache

i stand at the door trapped in her chatter
polite cordial well-behaved
on verge of scream

she's dead down there
decomposing in front of the television

the phone rings

"me very sick," she whines
"please please turn down the loud music"

THE RIDER

approaches his destination
sits still, one arm braced against the seat
he's tall young death lean. his clothes cling, disheveled
under them the white gaunt skeleton/man, translucent skin
tendons stretched tight
the anemic course of blue veins his face the tragic comic
mask of corpse/sunk cheeks prominent protrusion of neck
day's growth of beard, brown hair matted under
his awkward crown/a black flyer's cap too large
and as ill-fitting as the matching jacket
who is he? did they "do him in" in viet nam? or cancer
the metastatic horror eating him cell by cell
or devastating hell of self abuse, drugs, malnourishment or
insidious congenital disease/blood heirloom feeding on its progeny
or that white terror, poverty
he rides relaxed against the seat eyes closed
lips move silent shapings/a prayer/chant/litany or
name of one loved

THE LADY WITH BOUGAINVILLEA IN HER EYES

—for Kate Braverman

cries death her father
cancer eats away at the family
a brother who'd rather forget
memories of harsh words glisten like
garnets
cool crisp hospital walls close in
and mother, a shrieking harpy silenced by
pending shadow of the scythe, returns
thank you notes for flowers
oh, this mouth of pain
this moth that lunges to be free of cocoon
she enters, long black hair kissing worried shallow cheeks
in three-inch stacked heels, upon the stage
this poet-vamp clasps her arms at the elbows. in the
quiet of the lobby whispers "daddy you s.o.b. i love you"
and sinks into the folds of her heart
"keep fighting, we're all pulling . . ."
home, oh this house of pain
and in and out the neighborhood swoop
victims looking for victims/madness, the
furtive moon appears on her doorstep
threatening rape
and three blocks away the love of her life
drinks their future into oblivion
while she fights lust
for the needle's plunge, remembering
"daddy needs me to be straight"
and oh, the pain
would that she be in mexico, mainlining cocaine
languishing in the plaza of lost loves
her heart exploring catacombs of the dead
where she would go to meet her father
among conquerors

KATE

offers her breast/friendship
milk/failure of man love
red tortured lips/dead relations
her imperfect body scarred by births by weddings
                                        divorces
                                        funerals
hudu rituals of moon worship
flesh juju
blue eyes
come at me in dreams, scream between
aspirations: woman thigh
sighs. fingers run thru blood black hair
mushrooms acid cocaine celibate
seductress of homosexual boy believers in womb mouth
                        MOTHERfucker of all
passion. rape by fire/tongue
eat who can be eat/holy vanilla hit list
              (tired of holidays spent alone)
seeks that rare fare homo sapiens erectus aeternus
offers up her breasts/womanness
nipples hard ice cold rose
champagne and stars

FLY BOY

at the bar the talk turned to World War II

      "a trip, wasn't it," someone said.
      "man what was you in?"
      "the Navy and never saw water."
      "Marines."
      "you's leathernecks were some mean motherfuckers."
      "and you—over there so quiet."
      "i was in the Army Air Corps."

silence

      "that was tops. 'specially for a nigger. *the elite.*"
      "yep. we trained hard 'n thought we was big shit, man.
gonna fight Nazi. kick Jap ass. was we fools."
      "didn't know they let us fly during the War."
      "yeah, well we all got on the bus that day, loud talkin'
'bout how nice it was gonna be to kill a white boy legal."
      "and so?"
      "we was overheard. never did get off the ground."

silence

      "say man, did i ever tell you bout the time i seduced
the daughter of New York's underworld king pin?"

SWAN

1

little girl pick up those jacks

she leaves the house
$3.00 in her bra. no identification
going rough
winter everywhere. no place to fly
on the bus
she wears no panty hose
he sees all the way to china
at the bar, fends off guys who want it free
no pussy tonight, daddy
the red army marches

2

young lady jacked up and pregnant

she leaves the baby alone
$3.00 until welfare arrives. no food
    baby i've cum
    want more?
    as much as I can get
    not now. things to do. kids to feed
    how much
    that's fine. thank you
    i need to eat your meat
    next thursday
    fine

3

woman say daddy i need some jack

desperate. flutter of 300 green backs
he dissolves into her eye
drink on a starless night in a too red bar
she picks up her purse
clutches tight
out the door and into night
his eager footsteps follow
echoes her laughter
all she ever wanted was death by flight
to say
"i was up there with the birds"

when we met
he was an actor of
some degree
he was
also a connoisseur of
music and pussy
prior to that
in a dim dull past
he'd clerked and hinted
he'd once had the luck to be a kept man
when we split
he became a writer
over the span of years
shaped his life into an
8½" x 11" MS
which was published by the wind
on a page of the hollywood freeway
later on i heard he became bisexual
one day he came by to tell me he'd
become a nice pimp
for a brief moment he was my step-father-in-law
now he doesn't know what he is
a movie producer
is what he'd like to be
or a buck
wild and antlered in wyoming
if it were at all possible
he'd be blue eyed and blond
the last time
i saw him
he was between being
didn't know what he was
except caged
and bloodless

CHINESE DOLL

i cannot wake her, the son says. i've never seen her like this
    before

it is difficult to keep up with the fast ones. they flit
past and flash and show and the slow ones/impatient
can't wait to catch up

no catching up

and here is success the bottle and here is love the bottle and here is
understanding the bottle and here is beauty the bottle and here
is peace the bottle and

she's been drinking for 2 weeks, the son says. i cannot wake her

it is difficult to keep up with the fast ones. they soar
while down here grounded, the slow ones/impatient
can't wait to sprout wings

snatch the wind

she's out in the car, the son says. she won't wake and she can't walk

she's forty. her skin, porcelain yellow, eyes closed, the perfume of
scotch 80 proof fills the cabin of the car. i lift her from her son's
arms as he struggles with the flesh of his mother, the weight of her
    stupor
the torpor of her snore/groan. i lift her and brace my back and carry
her left arm across her stomach exposed to early spring air, her right
    arm
limp and flagging, free of string

coma. the paramedics are called. they come with the stretcher. there is a
hospital across the way for dolls like these. they repair them frequently
with some success

in a little while she'll be alright. really all right
the pieces will be returned to the factory

and recycled

DEAR MAMA (2)

she say that's what
mama's for

you don't know or maybe you do
time you couldn't buy us shoes and asked grandpa
for money. he sent you one dollar
i remember your eyes scanning the letter. the tears
you got us shoes somehow by the good grace of a friend
maybe you are hip in your old-fashioned oklahoma cornspun way

or the time we sat in the dark with no electricity
eating peaches and cold toast
wondering where you'd gone to get the money
for light

grandma named you lewana. it sounds hawaiian
not that bastard mix of white black and red you are
not that bitter cast of negro staged to play to
rowdy crowds on the off broadway of american poor

and she added mae—to make it sound *country*
like jemima or butterfly mc queen or bobbi jo
it's you. and you named us and fed us and
i can't love you enuff for it

you don't know or maybe you do
it hurts being a grown working black woman
branded strong
hurts being unable to get over
in this filthy white world
hurts to ask your parents for help
hurts to swallow those old beaten borrowed green backs
whole
hurts to know
it'll hurt worse if you don't

66

SAINT THERESA

i slept. she rose
went south skimming freeway enroute to bitter end
floor where old cracked wood
record player ten years of spin
groove 45 blues. few remember *bad bad whisky*
mouth slur laughter and shouts
eyes cry "murder me quick, i can't stand it"
just what she did
not exactly—manslaughter
defending herself she hit her lover
his head against the solid iron frying pan
the children chorused mommy daddy screams
could have done a year in prison
county keep all them babies
good woman, god fearing woman
loved her man, cradles his ghost between
pages of Bible. didn't mean to kill
just knock him out
drunk and with another woman
lenient judge
floor glistens waxed finish
she pours extra social security/milk
buys new baby things
and that night she returned manless to
the juke
where i woke up
soaked

UNDER ARREST

freeze. freeze! that's right! freeze before i take
your head off. freeze! come on and raise. raise those
arms. get 'em up. let me see you raise those arms. high
or i'll take your head off. higher. higher! or
i'll spill your blood all over the sidewalk

okay, up against the car. spread 'em bitch—spread 'em!
you see what this is, don't you? you see what this is
and there's a bullet in this barrel that's just waiting to
bite your back. now spread 'em and spread 'em wide or
so help me i'll send you to visit jesus

i ought to take you into an alley and bash your head
in. that's right! where's your id? now put your hands
behind your back. we're gonna give you some bracelets
to wear but they won't be diamonds. jeez i'd like to
stomp your ass. you saw those flashing reds

i almost shot you back there, you *know* that? when are
you people gonna learn, huh? you talk too much. that
makes me damn mad when you talk too much. i was ready
to put lead into your brain, you *know* that? shit makes
me damn mad. rather take you to the morgue

UNDER ARREST (2)

they were caught unawares. the police kicked down the door
another ghetto coffee klatch busted. needles, spoons, the
whole watermelon. it may be sex in the suburbs but that's
the easiest thing to get southtown (can get thigh when you
can't get nothin' to eat), bail fifteen big ones

"he won't fuck tonight. no he won't fuck tonight" she kept
going from bitch to bitch itching, telling us how she got
one of 'em in the groin before they busted her she busted his
nuts and we kind of smiled at her and bore her red diamond
breath and shared a smile, knowing if she'd done what she said
she'd be dead

they busted him on robbery, a local boy they knew all too well
and he had left alive too many witnesses—all except
the main one, who he put paper on. she was dead a few weeks
after testimony and even her christ-kissing parents believed him
innocent, as would anyone looking into those pretty smiling
browns

BAD

night at the taco house
he came in to rob the place
the waitresses were flush fear and tears
the guys sat around yammering
what he was doing caused some kind of disruption
he beckoned. i went over to his corner
he put the gun to my head, said
"empty the register"
the kiss deep hard cold against my temple
there was a click sound
if i move sudden i'm dead, i thought
and if i hesitate this clown might off me
and so i said, "shoot motherfucka or quit wasting my time"
there was surprised silence
then everyone broke into strained laughter
"it's a joke," he said, "you didn't cry like the other girls"
and there were slaps on the back and
cracks about my ice cool
and from that day till the day i quit
everybody kept their distance

I LIVE FOR MY CAR

can't let go of it. to live is to drive. to have it function
smooth, flawless. to rise with morning and have it start
i pray to the mechanic for heat again and air conditioning
when i meet people i used to know i'm glad to see them until
i remember what i'm driving and am afraid they'll go outside and
see me climb into that struggle buggy and laugh deep long loud

i've become very proficient at keeping my car running. i
visit service stations and repair shops often which is why
i haven't a coat to wear or nice clothes or enough money each
month to pay the rent. i don't like my car to be dirty. i spend
saturday mornings scrubbing it down. i've promised it a new
      bumper
and a paint job. luckily this year i was able to pay registration

i dream that my car is transformed into a stylish
convertible and i'm riding along happily beneath sun glasses
the desert wind kissing my face my man beside me. we smile
we are very beautiful. sometimes the dreams become nightmares
i'm careening into an intersection the kids in the back seat scream
"mama!" i mash down on the brake. the pedal goes to the floor

i have frequent fantasies about running over people i don't like
with my car

my car's an absolute necessity in this city of cars where
you come to know people best by how they maneuver on the
      freeway
make lane changes or handle off-ramps. i've promised myself
i will one day own a luxury model. it'll be something
i can leave my children. till then i'm on spark plugs and lug nuts
keeping the one i have mobile. i live for it. can't let go of it
to drive is to live

SILLY BITCHES INSTITUTE

the tank at sybil brand
wrists fresh tingle of just removed
handcuffs. body fresh tingle from
the matron's hands in my bra
and panties
standing against the wall
one more bitch crimey shook down
one more pair of gums & gams searched
one more vagina probed for contraband
one more chump on the rack
to be sent upstairs
before shut down

smoke. cigarette smoke. nervous smoke
she's never been to county jail before
that one over there, the mexican illegal
her belly full of baby
she's due for immigration and shipment back across the border
she cries in spanish

who's the meanest mean cunt
me and another sistuh
"what you in for?"
"dope bust. you?"
"tore up somebody's property."
strong ones. queens. if it's butch play butch
the white bird flies in solo
middle class, forty, never been in trouble
nice dresser and got ten bucks change
the fat bag of coins jingles as she bounces on stacked heels
into the tank 'n can't hide her shock
we SEE she's never been among so many niggers
her eyes solicit sympathy

it ain't here. there's no civil rights. no aunt jemima
no humanity

lamb baby, lamb

the wolves move in
two sistuhs help themselves. one grabs and holds
the other one snatches the sack of coins and her cigarettes
"leave me a dime at least!" she breaks into tears
"aw shut up, fool," somebody laughs
"won't someone help me?" her eyes catch mine
sorry, but in here the world is black

to the shower
and the pesticide spray for lice and other vermin
scum like me is bound to have in cracks and crannies
i turn in my civvies and get my issue: dress

> sweater
> what-the-fuck-are-these-
> shoes?

"damn niggah, you gots big feet!"
i'd like to put 'em up somebody's ass. hers will do

to the "makeup" room for mug shots and finger prints
numbers are assigned
washing the ink from my hands i'm told there's one more
cage to wait in and from there it's outside on bail
or upstairs

waiting. one by one we file in. the door is locked
again. someone coughs. someone fires a
cigarette. conversation is sparse
we wait to hear our names called
turn of the key means we're free to go
back home wherever and whatever home is

the lieutenant unlocks the door, calls

73

it ain't me
she gets up, smiles, she's going home
feels our envy, our stares
throws us a big goodbye kiss and splits
our eyes thru the glass pace out each step she takes
freedom/the release window
the lucky cunt

a half hour later she's back hurt angry
"they ran a make on me"
another warrant turned up and it's "scoot over ladies"

as we enter the elevator our "guide" the lieutenant
tall blonde neatly stacked greek curls catches my eyes
i won't look away
"you. i don't like your attitude. you stay
here long and you've got trouble"

upstairs the latins and whites are separated from the blacks

see women

they look like men
no makeup. no lotion. no scented soaps. no perfume.
no hairdos. as is. like after bath
ashy and itchy

clang. the cell door shut

cold black bars
my bunky a yellow overweight amazon
with ulcers on her legs and big purple bruises and blotches
won in a fight. her eyes the damage well done
one good, the other lost in swollen
blue-black flesh

lights out girls

sung to sleep to the lullaby of a
young black junky screaming for her monkey
laid back on my bunk
it's thin and its coils bite their way into memory

out mama. get me out of here

MURDER

by arson. the yente landlady
who keeps calling me up to tell me how much
she hates to evict us
for blacks, we're nice people

by mass gassing in ovens. the automobile
manufacturers of america who mated
the car to planned obsolescence

by hanging. my employer
who's figured out
how badly i need this shit job

by bullet. my lover and my girlfriend
who slept together over my dead body
then resurrected me for
parasexual trial

by starvation. my ex-husband
who never has a card or kind word
for his children

by poison. the me
who has faith in people

MEN LIPS

they smell of booze and come swaggering thru a barroom door
pressing eagerly for release—a pot to piss in

coughing up the spit of resentment. tight lines of i-love-yous
clipped short. curled under pressure

loose and slipping easy over. wet warm and juice flowing
flavor of mint

musty with musk—heady and eager to please
acceptance the tongue which finds its way between tight thighs

stretched from one pole to the next, vomiting
up word politics and little green things with knives

licking down around my question
a nervous lapping tells me he wants out

his on mine sucking inward. a palate formed of prison bars
he tastes like damp and unfamiliar alleys

BLUE SONG SUNG IN ROOM OF TORRID GOODBYES

1

big black mama wears a man's hat cocked on her head and when
     blue
belts out a song for all fast ladies to hear and nod
in soul felt empathy:

> why do we loves so the men
> what does us so wrong

> the gamblin' men what been
> in jail for crime

> fathers of our nappy headed
> brawling brats

> glorious low down motherfuckas
> every single one

> why do we loves so the men
> what always done us wrong

2

into blues skin
his body pierces—sweet

smell musty thighs
and matted kinky hair

oh they were good lovers every one

into chasm/seconal dream
he leaves for viet nam

a lucky piece of cannon fodder
he only lost his mind

oh they always stood so tall

and on the yard we'd promenade
make love standing up
a limey fuck behind the wall
balling beneath the gun tower

oh they always be chasin' other bitches

into green's jealousy
his body sound
deep into my womb
a jazz concert played

3

hooked on love
this jones won't leave her alone

        (he comes into her dream
        reminds her she used to suck his nipples)

hooked on love
rolls up her sheets takes the needle

        (he was too long. liked to
        hurt her stabbing with his dick)

hooked on love
she beats her breast in withdrawal/lonely

        (they used to talk. he liked
        her politics, her smile)

hooked on love
wrapped in agony/needs to be touched

        (a fellow iconoclast so rare
        warped genius they could be mad together)

hooked on love
looking for the antidose/another niggah

        (he listened to her plot
        her revolutionary tears. held her still)

        4

in deep
over his head
mouth spews curses
poison/racism
binds into a knot
flesh burns
spontaneous combustion
fuck friction
blue notes

in deep
over her head
heart betrays
poison/racism
binds into a knot
burns flesh
success's frustration
blue notes

in so deep
each morning a miracle

a blue note for unborn children

5

black man, arms too short
in suit, sleeves too long
too much brain
in skin, color too black/crimester

        nightcap we toast separate futures
        glass of akadama soul for him
        scintillating seven-up star for me
        arms wrapped at elbows eye-to-eye a pact

black man with pool cue
studies the table, a pro
silk to his hands, chalks up
"love into her side pocket"

        night feels
        roasting in our bodies
        our tongues exchange flames
        have eaten human flesh
        desire no other

6

sweet liquors do not wash away
the taste of his blood running thru my teeth

LOVE THE LETTERS

written in thin penned impermanent ink/a
young black woman's fever

pages yellow in sealed envelopes
how soon forgot the my love for you will never dies
how buried dust deep the
there will never be anothers
you are my lasts
i can't live without yous
buried with time and the apt shovel of experience

such comedy first love
love always
the dizzy spin/hyperventilated ache
torture and sweat of it
give all to give of it

letters/pain pressed thin from
storage for review
tell me how stupid i was then
and how stupid i remain

LESSONS

never get into a car with more than
one man

play dumb

if met with resistance, "act a niggah"

lie with your body
back it up with your eyes

pretend great hurt but don't cry

get high but never unaware

smile even if you can't stand it
tell him how good it feels

fake satisfaction

do not go into the pocket until he reaches
the third level of sleep

never go back to the crime scene

remember? we were here once. love was a new cut
of meat, the sweat of fresh blood. into each other's eyes
falling. a closeness of breath. a toast. two glasses. reflection
his knee courting mine. and i thought wrong. thought maybe

flesh time. widowed sheets. a memory of a half flushed toilet.
the smell of him lingers just at the edge of my nose. a pressed
carnation stains the paper of our lives. pages to lock away
in a chest of disquiet

where are they all now? the ones who listened so rapt to our
rhetoric? the spirits that mirrored my enthusiasm/lust for
        adventure?
the window that promised escape in case the smoke became too
        thick

a prayer catches me unaware. religiosity is something other than
dogma. the stink of our love losing potence between applications of
pine sol and i'm burning for him/bacon on a hot greasy grill

the singer sets a mood. what more can we do, we cemented in
        bond of
flesh, eager to get there, never tiring of the ritual: detergent and
bleach. the sun burning kisses on the tips of my fingers pressed
        against
safety glass. sometimes his touch comes through with the urgency of
a dying race: my heart beneath his shoe

we whispered overthrows, speculated on the egyptian book of the
        dead
soul train and liberation. whatever happened to the brown-eyed
me, a mini-skirted wound weeping soft red candle light? she
reappears occasionally behind motel doors, takes her
lover's wallet while he sleeps and steals away

DAY

dead white chill hand of the waker dispels dreams
brings horror

no i do not want to go out

winter awaits me in the light
it skitters. it booms. it knocks down
invades
slithers beneath the windows, tries to get in
surrounds
just outside pressed against dusty louvers
still. hulking. shimmery
i know it's there
a thing hungry icy cold cruel
a blast of arctic air that sears skin
the spiral mouth time sucks up years
howling phrenetic terrible
a dying wail

i hide from it here in the dark
shades drawn, tensed

OFFICE POLITICS

the white boss

stops at my desk to see how i'm doing. it's something, what a
good strong work horse i am. nothing like those lazy mexicans
and them power hungry jews can't be trusted
who knows what's on the oriental mind
but we negroes understand what the white man is about
we understand that his best interest is ours
that's why we've always made such fine employees

the jewish foreman

stops at my desk to say how's it going. we are soul mates
after all we have much more in common than other races
my slavery and his death camp. not like those greasy mexicans
or clannish orientals. there are jews in the NAACP
and Harlem was once a jewish ghetto
if it weren't for jews the negroes would be
worse off

the white feminist co-worker

brands men subhuman. as her black "sister" don't i understand
our oppression is the same? what is the difference
between being lynched and being man-handled?
and didn't white female abolitionists play a major role
in our emancipation? and black men are
the same as white men. they are men aren't they?

the mexican co-worker

confides outrage. the white boy's days are numbered
california & texas will be spanish-speaking again and soon

we will not allow the red herring of jobs
to set us at each other's throats. the white boy and
the jew can only buy the illusion of loyalty from us
never the reality

the japanese accountant

passes by my desk to his
does not say a word
when everyone else
is out of the office
save me and him
he goes into his attaché case
for the flask of scotch
and bottoms up
without offering me
a sip

my black co-worker

comes over to my desk. looks deep
into my eyes. opens his mouth. moans
shakes his head
and goes back to work

GROUND ZERO

the marauder is invisible
thunder of hooves against hard earth
unseen riders
everywhere newly orphaned children
we do not know who's responsible
there's no name to name
no object for the finger of guilt
no bloody hands
everything is spotless. well ordered
not a hair out of place
no sweat
buttons undisturbed
the streets are vacant
so strange this quiet war
so strange its respectable dead

listen. the blast is coming
a wingless dove
sent round the world
by endless greed

WHEN MY TIMES COMES

i will speak to the night. it will listen
words faint as breath
a door thru which i escape/another world

imagination carries me
i am light, float/smoke/waft
this dance on the killing floor of spirit

light one candle and move on

oboe my mouth turned inward
dream i am possessed by the dream: arrival

the fire
my skin peels off, beneath it soft moist black earth

mother the candle burns slow

communicate? it's hard to talk
difficult to sculpt

the flame gives off no warmth

the many ways i spell hate on every empty wall

when my time comes
i will speak to the night
it will rise
and follow

2

*funny thing. i couldn't give him a reason
not to stay high all the time*

FLIGHT OF THE CALIFORNIA CONDOR

for you, los angeles—you at my jugular

wind sistuh blooded eyes
mind full of flesh

> womb/dark moist
> unknown walls suck you
> so deep down
> you become lost
> die there

what the eyes tell him he senses, the way the rabbit pursuit
descent out of sky, claws/talons—*snatch*. he's
helpless, midair, familiar ground gives way this alien sky
ahead, the nest and death. he is fed to the young

breaker breaker
this is the hollywatts kid comin' at yah

steadily they grow. strong, vibrant, vital. they curl and
uncurl, test their environs. cry of discovery. something
inside hungers to wing free

> at the party the wealthy white bridge
> champion followed me from one chair to the
> next. "tell me what did I do? *what did I do?*
> the three black ones i loved hurt me
> what did i do? they took my money
> and left. why?"

here on this plain, constant thunder. no rain. the sky
seems pregnant, about to burst, enraged. but no. only the
splash-lash of lightning opening up corners of the room

93

dispelling shadows for a second. long into day it can be heard
for miles—thunder/the heart embedded in the groin of fear

at the office he came to tell me how much
we had in common. classical music,
writing, intelligence. "If
you'll forgive me, we must be soul mates,"
and in his eyes and in his wife's eyes the
mattress waited, convulsed with our flesh
entwined. taste of me on his tongue, and hers
what would it be like entering me, fucking
my soul. i said no. he tried to get me fired

wing spread like a condor. the multicolored feather coat. rare
bird this. it burns/an unanswered question, is as inaccessible
as the planet's heart, preens and struts, avoids capture. like the
horizon—is never reached

break into me, break into me
this earth has never been violated

it expands to welcome, closes
clangs/bolts/lockup
in county jail
imprisoned, he moves
to tear free

like quicksand, she appears harmless, ordinary, calm. he
didn't recognize until he was up to his nose in her, seeing
too late. either to be pulled suddenly, violently free or
expire in that hole

it labors. contracts. gives out.
screams dance in her lungs
pepper the page
so many ink blots/a drop

on him shrivels him up like
a slug under salt

"if i had known i was going to die in california, i'd never have
come here," his few belongings hastily packed. the guitar across
his back. taking a vacation, not knowing there would be nothing to
come back to except his old army picture dangling from the
        bedroom
wall. she would be gone and all traces of their life together

there's nothing delicate here. delicate
things do not survive. they get beaten up/raped/shot/
runover/knifed/poisoned or pushed into suicide
they harden, become brittle, or bend
baked under sun of years, adobe will not
yield to crop, but brick to build—
where the farmer fails, the architect prospers: a city

(one day we will plow you under and dance the ritual of your
        passing)

under quicksand she waits. how long before he discovers
it's a movie prop/emerges a bit confused, perhaps embarrassed but
alive to find the treasure of her embrace, test passed
successfully. but he drops to her feet a corpse/choked on fear
angrily she rewrites the script for the next actor

                i am dressed in a thin lavender negligee
                crouched behind the door. he moves past me onto
                the porch to see if i've escaped. spits a curse
                and stomps drunk, upstairs. i flee. the children/he
                won't hurt the children, can't hurt the children
                but he'll kill me so i run, feet bare against
                sidewalk/glass rock bottle cap bite my feet
                draw blood. i run to brother love's
                beat on his door until he stirs. he allows me
                sanctuary and the employ of his tub

break me open, break me open
white on the outside, rich warm chocolate inside

these streets are lean, familiar faces in bitter forms that
dot doorways, cluster at corners, weave along the walk. i know
the pimp, the pootbutt, the whore, the worker, the blind, the
cowboy, the ditty-bop, the gangster, the hype, the hustler, the
young whites who visit the old whites who couldn't make the
    flight
exiled, the ghetto becomes home

                the adjective bank is empty
                the seer's tongue ensconced in
                a coat of cryptic truths
                her fingers/talons wet with
                blood of capture
                having plucked him from
                the desert's floor

mother of angels let me burn forever in the oven of your love

DOCTOR'S REPORT

patient complains of social dysfunction related to color

symptoms: homicidal/suicidal tendencies
                 erratic episodes of deep depression
chronic intermittent unemployment requiring outside financial
assistance (beg, borrow, steal)

past history: patient is a young black female divorcee with
                 two children. she is alert and cooperative
one moment and sullen and resentful the next. she states that
the complaint which brings her here today is on-going since birth
she also states she has seen other physicians in the past and
although they agree that she "does have something" they were
unable to determine its etiology

examination: patient exhibits emotional instability, for
                 example, crying and laughing at the same time
other mood swing observed encompassed hope to anger; an
insatiable hunger expressed by the patient as a "desire for freedom
and power of self-determination." this phenomenon has no
apparent physiological source

recommendation: institutionalization

97

AT VITAL STATISTICS

hard to breathe
hard to sit
processed

minutes stretch into day's wait
the broadness/discomfort
of flesh in the pockmarked expanse
of beige tiles and rows of chairs stamped "recorder"

part of me follows the blue line
and part of me, the red

zombies stagger through doorways/slips
of paper in hand
conjured up by clerical hoodoos
hidden pasts
loved ones married buried born

daydream: passing through the exit down the escalator
            that does not work to the grey cement
            regions where stilled autos
            await ignition

in this mausoleum the hum of impatience
confinement
boredom
vague rustle, a newspaper read a dozen times
makes its way to the floor

it's done by computer. no mirrors here
this strange magic of certification/proof
of existence (we do not live until our papers
are stored, our numbers assigned)

SHOP OF SIGNS

i sit in my father's dream
paint and turpentine smells
twenty year struggle to create a business
be someone in this big hick redneck town
proprietor/owner of/builder of scope/dimension
his net, brown fingernails caked in dirt and dust
hands disproportionate under the tumor's growth
and his eyes losing sight
it stinks, pops. how do you stand it?
he does not stop/does not give in to
blindness/miseducation/lack of
knowledge about how they do things
in white corporate america
and i would change him, naive as he was
when he came here in thirty-one
two years before the big quake
and thought he could shake this city too
young black boxer not good enough for
golden gloves, found a woman
settled into love and took up the brush
these forty-five years past have changed both maps
his, the city. i've watched them prosper/pain
papa, how do you do it?
i grow bitter by the day/pollution
strangles effort
my net, fingernails broken and bitten
belly grown disproportionate
with child. my eyes see too much
i want to stop. can't

WANDA & STEVE

at the comedy store

the italian clown had his act together until he decided to
use the couple up front as foils
    "how does it feel to be an interracial couple,"
he asked loudly from the stage.
    "we're not," the wife said.
    "that's right," said her husband.
shaken, the clown was unable to continue his routine and
the new act came on

after interviewing them

the white producer listened silently as the jewish producer
told the couple she couldn't use them

    "you're white," said the jewish producer.
    "i'm not white," said the husband.
    "well, you look too white. we're in business. people
might think you're an interracial couple and get hung up in
that. the film is about young couples adjusting to their new
babies and not social commentary. we don't want to have to
worry about distribution."
    after the two women film-makers left, the two of them
stood in the center of the room and hugged each other for a
very long time

at the restaurant

the pale blonde hostess asked them to "please wait a minute."
there was one empty table. a tall white brown-haired man
came in and stood behind them. the hostess returned and escorted
him to the table. she got upset and began to create a scene.

he tried to calm her down as they left to find some other place
for breakfast

on the beach

they walked up the boardwalk, smiling and talking, watching
the kids rollerskate. they strolled past the bench where
two black winos were trying to attract stray pussy. one called
out to her
    "hey, whore!"
    the husband put his arm protectively around his wife. she gave
the wino the finger

on their way to the bank

the man in his economy car pulled up along the curb and yelled
    "traitor!"
    "was that for you or me?" the husband asked.
    "must've been for me," the wife said, "the man was black"

ABOUT GOD & THINGS

1

i want to have your child
cuz upon losing you
i'll have more than memory
           more than ache
           more than greatness
i'll have laughter

i do not mean to be fatalistic
know the limits put on you black man
me, black woman

when you are killed or imprisoned
desert or separate from me
i'll continue
fill the void of your absence with
love between me and ours

gods

2

you love me
in your eyes. don't say it loud
pain
america will never let you

3

you're home. it's a surprise
you've made it thru another day
one more night in your arms
to fuck

merge our bodies merge
give
wealth/freedom
congress cannot legislate away

4

eyes wide as suns inquire
where's daddy?

he's gone away

i love my daddy

i smile
he's a good man

eyes wide as suns
burn my hand with a kiss
go outside to play in the streets

god
what god is about

TELEVISION STORY

it waits to be tuned in

she wants to do something else—dinner and a movie
or a drink at some club
there's not much they can afford

he wants to go trip with his brothers
they've copped some blotter acid
"there's been nothin' this good on the streets since '70"

she doesn't know how to tell him she hates it
when he does acid
it makes his fucking erratic
plus it's something she won't share cuz she's pregnant
she wants to stay clean

he promised to keep his system drug free
until conception
she can't lay that trip on him anymore

she tells him go. be with his brothers
that's what he wants
she resents it
he feels her resentment. doesn't react
he frenches her with passion. she tries to be cold

she listens to the door shut
goes over to the bed and takes off her muumuu
in the mirror her belly full of child distended round fat
gobs of dimpled cocoa flesh
fat climbing upward settling into her face and neck

"he can't stand to look at me," she says aloud

she puts her muumuu back on
leaves the room
returns with a plate full of bread butter avocado cheese ham and
potato chips and a glass of chocolate milk

she comes over
picks up the program. looks. she finds something
turns the dial. it feels her touch
comes alive
it's her in front of it all night long

love

THE WAIT

pregnant and bruised inside
ahead hours standing in lines
forms to fill out
assistance
records to acquire
murder on feet

sitting for hours. the ass
sleeps. womb quakes. ears, alert (they may
call me any minute) six people ahead of me

i am hungry
if i go get something to eat
i might miss my name

pray to be called
pray to the book of state and federal regulations

       forgive me my difference
       that i be granted eligibility
       receive enuff money
       to pay rent
       restore utilities
       repair the car
       kill the twitch in my
       left eye

I CARRY THE MOON

my legs bend shake ache under the weight
it rumbles and rolls, is alive
and my back burdened with
excess pounds of brown, complains
days grind past and the moon ripens slow
rises like dough in my womb
i'm tired of waiting
suitcase packed, ready
cab fare tucked away
coaching the kids on what to do
should it fall to earth too soon
father-to-be listens eager
the stethoscope for heartbeat
the moon kicks, spins
restless inside
anxious to be

GIVING BIRTH

against bone. rubbing. pressure against bladder
i pee and pee and pee
and drink water and more water. never enough water
it twists in my womb
my belly a big brown bowl of jello quakes
twenty pounds and climbing
eat eat eat. milk. got to have ice cold milk
vitamins and iron three times daily
cocoa butter and hormone cream
infanstethoscope
sex sex sex. can't get enough of that funky stuff
bras getting too small. is that me in the mirror?
it bucks/brings belches
smooth skin. glossy hair. strong nails
i'm 99% body. my brain has dissolved into
headaches tears confusion
my navel sticks out/eye of cyclops
my life for an apple fritter
snipping the elastic in panties, another pair ruined
nausea. vomit. muscle strain
"they" tell you to eat fresh fruit and lots of
vegetables. eating fresh fruit and lots of vegetables
afraid of what it will/won't be
anxious. it's got to look like him
it's got to look like me. be healthy. be live. be all right
why doesn't it hurry up and come
read books. more books. know the tv program by heart
fantasies about returning to slim
the ass sleeps. tingles when wakened
walking is hard. sitting is hard. sex, an effort
he stands in lines for me
thirty pounds and climbing
people smile, are sympathetic

will it be capricorn or aquarius?
can't drive. too big to get behind the steering wheel
ice cream cone jones
(out of three hundred deliveries this year, ours
is his third legitimate, says doc, "it's what
they are doing to the black community")
daily reports to the grandmothers
is that me in the mirror?
he worries. i worry. we worry together
more hugs and affection
i can't reach my feet
more calcium and iron
wow. my gums are bleeding. scurvy?
it rubs. twists. kicks. moves
sex? it takes too much out of me
the flu. food poisoning. cold
too tight pants bite me
preparation: pelvic spread vaginal walls widen
forty pounds and climbing
showers. no more long hot luxury baths
muumuus and mules. naked = relief
his ear to my stomach to hear the heart beat
emergency cookies
it presses against my diaphragm. it's hard to
breathe. can't sleep good. dreams
more dreams. it's a boy. it's a girl
backaches. swollen feet
refrigerator lover, clandestine rendezvous at 2 AM
advice from the experienced, questions from the barren
the planets are lining up in scorpio
suitcase packed and ready
names for him. names for her
(everybody-else-we-know-who's-pregnant-is-having
a-perfect-baby pressure)
sex? oh yeah. used to be fun
it turns. kicks. twists

that's me in the mirror, definitely
why doesn't it hurry up and come
crying jags. throb of false labor
will he be there
when it's time?

SWEET MAMA WANDA TELLS FORTUNES FOR A PRICE (2)

a former life
my body recalls
coughs, spits up
after-birth
past events
dim as
pain fades

dark brown hole
sewn shut
crimson stains
signal healing
i'm hungry

food carts rattle
pushed by green smocked
attendants
moans. other mothers
other rooms

little thing is brought in
nourishes from my breasts
i smile
i hold him

i know what tomorrow
is all about

I SWEAT I MOP I STINK

try to keep it together
clean. well worn path a swath of soap
sponge elbow grease. days shine bright as
fresh polished silver and spotless imported crystal
nights are sporadic battles with waterbugs and roaches
a stray cat scouting garbage through the screen door
i spend hours chasing dust motes with rag or broom
coaxing cobwebs from corners
easing wrinkles out of the bedspread
old ragged poor neat
order keeps sane combatting chaos
books stacked precisely and lined up
in cases. each picture, ashtrays, magazines just so
lamps tilted at proper angles
deodorized toilet, floors swept, shelves tidy
taut sheets, smiles in place
faces washed and asses wiped

WHERE HE IS

blue night full of empty streets/my eyes
scan. any movement. any man. my man. his walk
he's out there. i wait without waiting
hungry. expectant. hot
with the memory of how he feels
between my thighs the damp sweat of other nights
tossing restless in the sheets between fantasy and flight

where is he?

blue night full of moon and palm trees
shadows cast/men move down avenues/sharp footsteps echo
rubber heeled renegades/a mindless romance of bodies
needing sex money pleasure
my eyes follow. register
always, the memories of how he feels
to be satisfied in the damp sweat of night
tossed starved in sheets or sprawled across the floor

where did he go?

(defiance is decision: sleep. sleep the sleep of the dead
i pretend i don't hear him when he comes in. pretend that his
question remains unuttered. pretend that his cool arms
have not reached out for my warmth or his lips pressed against
the back of my neck, moist and biting into it. pretend the
physical plane doesn't exist. that i am pure energy and his
hard dick entering me is a single beam of light)

where in the fuck is he?

blue bright morning full of purple hills/sunrise
light spring wind and roses. smell of bacon & hot coffee

113

i wake without waking. full
complete. snuggle up to memory
how he felt between my thighs still damp
with last night's sweet sweat good
the sheets tossed back and singing, a towel
for mop-up-after stuck between my thighs

and there he is

on the pillow next to me curled up and snoring

DREAM 13

he fell into a pool of yellow stuff and spiders
that was after the chase. after the
hit man had been made. after the girl who made it
the first time failed to make it the second
blood/a mirror of cracked glass
impression: people running. most of them
black men in business suits. my oldest brother
i see his face. he is running. i am
running. to the parking lot. for the get-a-way
cars. the staircase piss poor narrow
above, i see the hit man as the body thuds past
into sticky spiders. at home in the
mail box an insurance check/someone's
blood on my hands. i will bank it right away
into the low hung chevy. it starts
radiator trouble. into the service station
for water. the latin boy opens
the glove compartment, sees the automatic in its
leatherette. brazen, steals it
opens it, admires it, fires a shot
it's returned to me by the station owner
i explain my husband gave it to me for protection
crime and all. the police want to know where
the acid stains on the hood come from. what
acid stains? i ask as i slip off into consciousness
and the baby's cry

MOOT

night the pillow cups me. want
i lay silent wait to hear him come in
and fall asleep. he comes but don't wake me

at the club the floor's alive with couples
i sit there in my drink
he talks to the guy in the next chair

in the theatre the screen is all love and surrender
embrace and music swells
he offers popcorn and a straw for the coke

naked wet dripping
after bath i come in my hair wrapped in a towel
he sits, smokes and thumbs thru the stereo catalog

she is prettier. my eyes follow his along her body
when he finds her crotch
i look away

MY LOVE BRINGS FLOWERS

a bouquet
for all the reasons
he does not have to give

it's material things make married so hard

i make one chicken feed five
make clothes ten years old fashionable
rejuvenate one fake sable coat

poverty endows one with magic

(how to do without turns garden to weed)

basil and blackthorn
my voice i have no thing

henbane and wild thyme
i scrape bottom

nettle and rye
i sweep out dead dreams

plum buds and tamaris
i promise the kids

moss and china asters
i borrow from friends

ivy yucca and wild rue
dark empty arms

money be as mad as you can afford

poor demands be alert, on the dime, sane
clumsy moment, a week's pay gone. too heavy a foot
$70 in brake repairs. a forgotten pill is $400
to abort. soon they'll corner the market on air
i'll gasp and curse my skin
unable to breathe

(ganja takes the stiff out, wine cuts the knot)

he comes in with a bouquet of smiles
i love him for the first time again
down to dirty sheets and stinky socks
down to unpaid bills and beans 4 times a week
to the bone
to the blood rose

REASONS WHY

eyes from green to red
cigarette trails a half inch ash

distant. cry of the baby/his image

he's silent as the lights go out/a
fist of dark closes round

flesh. we sleep naked. close

want you

doesn't happen can't happen
hungry
for something—get high

says
babe i can't find a job
didn't get those classes i wanted

need you

holds me tight
his mind somewheres off

love you

another smoke
and somethin' i don't know

he can't be a man tonight

SNAKES

secrets coiled, ready to strike/bite
his eyes into my eyes
hold me
then move off slow
our conversation casual
my ear has heard/knows his mood/hiss/warning
blood chill. i sit still
concentrate on no sudden moves/our life
how long
before the venom reaches the heart?

there be a devil in the house
it steal money and put it in the vein
it come tip-toe thru the door
i hear him try to catch him
but he too slick
locks don't keep him out
or drum

STEPHEN'S MONKEY

it shits on the curtains
scampers out of my angry reach

its cool moist skin and tail
holds wide brown blank eyes to flesh, passes
between this world and the next/nods
who goes there and what hope
what vacant hole yawns/canyons
the arms, veins bursting with fluid
stare forward and stare back
i enter the room fresh on his trail
bed down next to his snore
rise to find him in last night's leftover coffee
he goes there but barely there
like take five like street light
like the dust that settles on this page
he tips in
quiet as time
goes for the bathroom
for the rubber hose
the stuff

RAPE

—thanx, Kika Warfield

i am here to help you

he laughed. and his partner laughed. she squeezed
her palms/triggers. their uniforms bled
the laughter became screams of horror and she
dragged the bodies of the white blond cop and
his chinese bunky down stairs
and buried them in her eyes/hatred
sprang up and blossomed

talk about it

tell me every detail, said the doctor
they broke in on me. every detail. they took me
in the bedroom, one at a time. next detail
i was scared they'd find my purse—i lied about
having no money. detail, detail. they undressed me,
asked me to tell them how it felt. did it feel
good? yes. did you cum? they were gentle lovers
did you cum? yes. both times? yes

the boyfriend

came in. she was feeling shrunken dirty suicide
she hadn't douched. the wetness still pouring
out/a sticky riverlet on her inner thighs
he got indignant. why didn't she call the police
why didn't she call her mama. why didn't she die
fighting. she remained silent. he asked her where
it happened. she showed him the spot. he
pulled down his pants, forced her back onto the sheets

122

i haven't cleaned up, she whined. but he was
full saddle hard dicking and cumming torrents

the two burglars

kicked the door in. she woke. she thought, he's
drunk again. she slipped into her thin pink
gown, got up and went to see. it wasn't him. we
have guns, the dark one announced
there's no one here but me and the kids she said

there was little

for them to steal. the dark one took her into
the bedroom while his partner searched. he turned
out the lights and stripped. he laid her gently on
the bed. this is my name. when you cum, call
my name. she agreed. and he entered. your pussy's
hot and tight. where's your old man? he's
a fool not to be here with you. you're pretty
you're soft. you fuck good. kiss me. and she did
as told. we don't want to hurt you. you like
the way i kiss. tell the truth. it's good,
she said and after a while she moaned his name

the other one

came in and took off his clothes in the dark
i'm really sorry to do this, he said, but
i can't help myself. strange, she thought. such
polite rapists. i wonder if they'll kill me
somehow i must make them care enough not
to kill me. he told her his name and sucked
hungry at her nipples, parted her legs
he was very thick long hard. his friend's seed
eased the pain. i want your tongue he said

give me your tongue. she gave and gave
jesus! he cried and shot into her, long spastic jerks
he trembled and fell into her arms. shit
that was good

in the kitchen

her few valuables were piled neatly mid-floor
she promised not to call the police
what could they do, save her?
the other one, the jesus-man took her typewriter
and put it back, and all the other stuff they
had planned to take. even the television

here is my number, said the dark one
when you get lonely, call

and she walked

them to the door. the dark one took her in his arms
kissed her goodbye

she waited

until she was sure they wouldn't
come back and kill

she picked up the phone

and made the mistake of thinking the world
would understand

THE READING

they came down to see my tragedy
one of those bloody nights
the streets were hot gray
i summoned familiar faces from all over L.A. and
vomited all over myself right before their eyes

> (it may not make for good living, she said
> but it sure makes wonderful poetry)

he was there, had a front seat in my heat
i foresaw our night together knew it would be good
it was. we fucked like no tomorrow
at 2 AM he sneaked out and didn't bother to lock the door
i could've been murdered in bed

> (yeah, she said, i wouldn't do that for the world
> you're stronger than i am. you can take it)

summer into his eyes
his tongue i missed yous in my ear, along my neck
it wasn't love but damn i was content to make do
should've known better should've smelled a rat
been deserted by so many
times i couldn't even get a decent put down

> (what'd it feel like? i'm a mindfuckin' yoyo
> of a voyeur. feed my pain long distance)

i lay there blood on her rug
memories spilled out of me a funky torrent of blues
i'd be lucky to be strung out on something tangible
like heroin or speed
there must be something illegal i can do

125

(give me all the details. i don't want to miss
a thing, she squeezed the siphon)

when he ignored me at the party
i decided it takes a niggah to forget a niggah
even that one's in texas now. brother love near sends
me to the hospital when we get down
do people die of over copulation?

(give me a rag girl. give me a rag. let me plug
up that hole fo' you drown me, sugar)

AFTER THE POEM

a stunned audience silent as 4 AM avenues
i walk home alone
in the still awesome morn's cold
climb dark steep stained gold carpeted stairs
to more silence graced by
dream breath of children, the
hum of the refrigerator's stubborn motor
and restless ghosts

where is he
why isn't he here
i have answers/memories/regrets
madness

i have
iced sheets. 2 pillows. slow jazz knife into my heart
i have
a bottle full of wine. coke in a thin crisp envelope
and marijuana

where are you
why aren't you here

i have a book. a tv program. a pen
the phone numbers of friends
mother and brothers

once upon a time his hands guide me thru hallways
talks sweet nothings maybes forevers
our eyes cathedral wide
he rolls the smoke, fires it, puts it to my lips
a toke, we kiss, he fires me
once upon his hands in my blouse finds nipples

his hands in my jeans finds wet
my tongue in his ear whispers. my hands in his
slacks finds firm welcome

once into each other
it was all right

mr. & mrs. lost & found
we spoke the same tongue

after our poem
the world was bearable

AFTER THE POEM (2)

we drive in from Golden Gate City
the host and i share a joint/silence
my thoughts break against safety glass, shatter
i smell my blood
can't stop the blood
kind, the host sees and says nothing
what can you do for the dead
but ease their journey
he passes the smoke. i take a draw
we cross the Bay Bridge into a quieter time
stoned euphoric pain, i
ease out into cold night, enter sanctuary
retreat to my bunk, a mess
the host retires
alone, i open up my chest, cut out my heart
stop the flow

STORM CLOUDS

wet against my neck
rain/tears of my children
tug at my skin/dreams mama can't fulfill
out here on the damned avenue
waiting for a bus ride home
my tongue against my teeth/wired
on pills to prevent pregnancy
pills to melt away the fat
marijuana to tone down lack-of-money pressures
rain against me beating hard as my heart
wet my shoes wet my pants wet my face
shivering in the cold as it
brings on the flu

WORKER

the lean months drag on/legions
of faceless men in a
calendar of lies
paydays/duns/debts

one by one i cross them off
burdens peel away/layers of skin
chapped cracked bitten
under sun/wind/finance
i farm the barren soil of city

my legacy the taut noose,
a stern plow, intolerant cotton—a harvest
of slaves & share croppers
mine eyes have seen the horror

they tug at me, the children
persistent at hem of my weary skirt
we must eat. we must have shelter
we must

live. out of my hand/sweat/bread
scheme. no time to idle in
green pastures or chase stray dogs
through daisy laden fields

i must

mark off each day one more mouth fed
one more bed made
one more penny pinched
one more diaper flagging in sunshine

at night those stars too far away
come down, light my pillow
i put my feet up, lay back
catch a dream

one more day. one more victory

GOOD MAMA

i've tried so hard to be good
looking at all these good years
good to people
good to you
true and blue to my ideals
good mama. do you hear me? so motherfuckin' good!
good cook
good mother
good sister
good friend
good love
remember everybody's birthdays and send cards
and call every now and then or drop a line to let them know
i care
good mornings
good nights
try to please and help and aid and
good mama
be responsible to god the father my country and help my
poor enslaved people
good mama. so fuckin' good. out good all the rest
oh so damnable good
good to death

EVICTION

no money. no place to go
who must i kill tonight to live
against wall of my skin
a line-up beneath harsh zeon
atmosphere: stale cig smoke, coughs, spilt coffee
behind bars women lose softness
sex is barter
extracted in eyes
he's doing the best he can to bail me out
this is it—*real* estate
exiled to the cage
this nightmare is pain precious
better than nothing

THE ONE WHO CAN

morning. he sleeps a dead sleep
her eyes follow his dream/rapid eye moves
boy/adult/cipher

no place

she grits under weight of his pain
how far before she breaks how far
tears/laughter/cries/strained silence

no purpose

they've fried him again
how many months unemployed? he reverts
to type: street cronies/winos/"good guys"
dominoes in the rundown upstairs haven for scum bums

thins out

limp. bent. beat
he looks out dirty windows/the world
lights the day's eleventh cigarette
it's tough. to keep love alive
he wants to do great things for her and the kids/MAN

no job

try goddamn try goddamn try
walks the streets
easier to walk out. vowed better-worse
too rare the better. can't get much worse

no point

morning. no waking
the nightmare goes on

and she
goes on the one who can

does

FELON

my heart comes thru my skin

they've snatched my kids

if the police catch me home i'm sunk
(when handcuffed the first and greatest itch
is my nose)

better find some place to spend the night
the car
sleep behind the wheel behind the
apartment building in winter night cold
doors locked
i wake but the scream goes on

can't tell mama about this

crimester. only crime i'm guilty of trying to
play alice straight in crookedland

money bitch. can't get hold of it

if the cops stop me it's jail without bail
drive. careful. one eye on the road
one eye on the rear view. one eye on tomorrow

help   county hospital psycho ward
        the gay psychiatrist tells me "write a book"
        my employer saves my neck cuz it's his wallet
        his attorney thinks i'm a cut above scum
        the foster mother smiles beneath her black bouffant wig
        and tells me my children are well behaved

court   the judge is black-robed and pleasant
              nods. extenuating circumstance (so rare to see
              a nigger here on somethin' other than homicide dope
              prostitution rape robbery)
              yes
              the records are sealed

they almost took me out this time

provide he said. provide
the condition of my release/getting them back
in my custody

i must provide (try to make a dollar outta 15¢)

i will. with difficulty
but i will

138

'TIS MORNING MAKES MOTHER A KILLER

mean

the day grinds its way slowly into her back/a bad
mattress stiffens her jaw

it is the mindless banalities that pass as conversation
between co-workers

her paycheck spread too thin across the bread of
weeks; too much gristle and bone and not enough

blood

meatless meals of beans and corn bread/nights
in the electronic arms of the tube

mean as a bear

carrying groceries home in the rain in shoes
twice resoled and feverish with flu

it is the early dawn

mocking her unfinished efforts; unpaid bills,
unanswered letters, unironod clothes

tracks

of pain in her face left by time; the fickle high of it
facing the mirror of black flesh

mean as mean can

pushed to the floor but max is not max enough
no power/out of control/anxiety

it is the sun illuminating cobwebs

that strips her of her haunted beauty; reveals
the hag at her desperate hour

children beware

AFTER WORK

he comes by to see me
we eat and talk with the kids
and watch television
or go out to a movie
and beneath it all, tensions
why he can't come back like before
why i can't take being bumped anymore
two lean dogs hungry for the fat of a pig's life
livin' black/stuck on the bottom/burnt
but we don't talk about those transitory things
we drive up the hill
and hold hands as we look out
at all the million lights spelling los angeles
in breath stopping panorama
and then we fuck in the front seat
of his brother's car
like guilt driven teenagers
crazy in love

REHABILITATION

take one tiger
remove from jungle
file down teeth and claws
zoo
tranquilize, feed, observe
for indeterminate period of time
when finished
return to jungle

JUNK

he poured out the pills, soaked them
drew the fluid into the syringe
shot up our future

he got hooked
money ran short
tracks marred the sheets

he couldn't share it

acid
we watched moonrise and stars pepper echo park
wishes dance in platinum plate glass
smoke
we shared a joint and our ears
music loud as the neighbors could stand it
opium
burned my cheeks and fired his and our dreams
water splashed to the coals of our flesh/steam
cocaine
and chatter and noses sniffing at mirrors, well strawed
for hours preoccupied with selves/stories
mushrooms
chewed with fresh orange or honey over ice cream
vision: the promise to the meek kept

babe my heart was in that Rx

        some of us have to have order
        lives neatly tucked in like the corners of a bed
        well dusted shades and polished table tops
        rooms where even the air is at attention
        lives like sculpted shaped bronze
        reasons so many neat well scrubbed children

with perfect manners and white socks
some of us have to have work
hard driving labor that draws sweat
purifies body, soul, mind, exhilarates
labor that sates in its accomplishment and
rewards
some of us must have a singular love
in or out of hipness
some of us must

there's no glory in the needle

she kicked it in the desert
at 90 miles an hour
she kicked it right in its beautiful black face
right in the crotch
right where it hurt the most

IN THIS WAKING

he walks the blistered boulevards for hours
hunting work
he goes in and out of restaurants
when he comes home he smells of smoke
and hot kitchens

she waits for the phone to sing/good news
if he gets the gig there'll be money for food dope rent
and the possibility of escape from hell

he smokes hemp. they smoke it together
and time and skin and rhythm merge
there is the drum and the hunger
a baby is made at his request

she finds work but doesn't have the strength
he thought would save them
and he doesn't have 400 years of patience

he's too good, she thinks. something is wrong
the walls tell her. and there is

he's developed an itch in his armpits

she walks the ledge
he has the choice of rescue
or taking her for the fall
one day she finds his goodbye
in the mailbox

and as she strikes cement she is certain
the shattered pieces of her sanity
will forever steal his sleep

venetian blinds/his eyes
i am buoyant and filled with dreams

smoke occludes thought
i cannot find me/grope

this opiate, love—take a little
the cells sing

every orifice is open to him
she closes round him/earth

the strange animal struggles in the pit
cries. extinction

who are we who mark the demise
who herald the birth

black as tar
black as jazz
pitch

who exorcise the new age
as if it were demon

children, your song transcends me
i am gone

6:50 PM. THE PHONE RINGS. IT'S HIM

within the context of our lives
it could never happen

       you bring out the woman

complete opposites. this city would
kill you slow and sure
i'd be little help
this poverty/my life/blackness
you'd die in the cage of it
a felled white sparrow

       i wanted to be better for you
       fuck you silly

here in this dim room
my bottle of wine and i
my bottle of wine

i drink and remember your flesh
penetration/hard to orgasm
waves of relief washing over me
i trembled
i wanted to die in your arms

       i won't lie
       won't tell you you were the best

like on furlough
like on leave stateside: soldier boy & hooker w/a heart of gold
this is a different kind of war and i too am a soldier

one night is eternity

and so i can say it
and mean it

        i love you forever

cosmic love
like light

it will go on without absorption

i will sing your name
a mantra against loneliness & false love

billy

PRISONER OF LOS ANGELES (2)

in cold grey morning
comes the forlorn honk of workbound traffic
i wake to the video news report

the world is going off

rising, i struggle free of the quilt
& wet dreams of my lover dispel
leave me moist and wanting

in the bathroom
i rinse away illusions, brush my teeth and
unbraid my hair
there're the children to wake
breakfast to conjure
the job
the day laid out before me
the cold corpse of an endless grind

so this is it, i say to the enigma in the mirror
this is your lot/assignment/relegation
this is your city

i find my way to the picture window
my eyes capture the purple reach of hollywood's hills
the gold eye of sun mounting the east
the gray anguished arms of avenue

i will never leave here

I HAVE WATCHED THEM COME BACK TO THE VILLAGE

slain or broken, crippled or bent
        in defeat or madness
have wept and moaned with the others
        uttered prayers
danced endless hours to ward off the enemy
        who stalks us
i too have spent hours in the hut of the
        witch doctor
discussing one herb or another, potions, spells
        some juju to shield
runners have returned rabid with messages
        of doom and horror
i also closed my ears but my heart sat
        among my teeth
i have remained motionless so long fat
        and time mock me

            now everything tastes the same
            now all moons are gray
            now even the face of love is ugly

today i dance the war dance. today
        i ready my weapon

            it is time to triumph or die

M'SAI

i lay at his jaw—the lion
stub of my spearhead
i struggle
the beast before me
my flesh torn
blood
against my face
pain
throbbing
the beast eyes ablaze
i lash out
pain
screams/roars
have lodged my spearhead into his jaw
he drips blood
one of us victor/victim
my beautiful enemy
i admire the gold of his mane
insane bravado of the warrior
generations
of red & black men bred me
i shove
he roars
backs off
pain
i scramble away
am safe
must find witch doctor
my enemy has tasted of my flesh
next time
only one will
walk

IMAGOES

1

white birds do not eat them   (to get out
they taste bitter   or dry up
                                 here in this
drops from the air. blood   slag grey limbo)

wings for casting spells
crisp thin splashes of color
ground up fine: juju
a lover will speak true
or
cocoons in his food
spirit of blood rush enters
there will be many babies
fat and cocoa happy

                   wings spread
           against glass. wings. to be free
               wings on night
        wings against my face. my skin screams

white birds do not eat them

2

                                 phobia

butterflies in the jar
the child imprisons them. watches
delights. colors. "they eat lettuce," another
child smiles, "put holes in the lid so they can breathe"

in morning's dew a burial
she puts the tiny winged things amid green leaves

3

moths/souls of the unhappy dead

(the dog chases them across the field
stunned by the mad beating of black wings, retreats)

4

inside my stomach flutter winged dreams

no future. baby ails. husband, eyes glazed high nods out
children in heat/puberty/poverty. they want
the walls stink. mildew. smudged dark dirty mirrors
bruised flesh. she bleeds. dissatisfied
vein/mouth opened up and spurting

5

in the dark room
i listen to him undress
pants drop to the floor
he pulls back the sheets his
cool touch my warm ready
his hands to my waist
inside i flower. he finds me. alights
his proboscis uncoils
deep into me
sucks up

6

against my face the flutter

what's wrong
there's something in here. flying around
it's nothing

i hear it
go back to sleep
i'm afraid
keep still
i felt it come at me
a dream
no. something real

      7

(who comes to the sleeper in midnight city skin)

cocaine lumin white it flits thru night
feathered antennae
cool air. caress the light/my body calls
pain on return

                    the steel cocoon
                    carries me down slick streets
                    on my way to the end of the line
                    the door open

my red skin
great great grandmama walks the trail of tears

                    the white powder
                    carries me down silk sheets
                    on my way to the end of the line
                    my nose open

tonight i dance dance of dead
my ancestors enter
my body spins/shock
transmuted

my brown skin

great granddad makes the oklahoma land rush

slave of city
i bow before the ashes
the cold black tar my skin sticks
each move agony
i can't get out of it

fuck me. make it hurt

8

lost

heart valves the blood flow slows
eyes haunted eyes see beyond the veil

outside the window. let me in. i'm cold
my fists sore my blood cakes

the skin becomes translucent, glows
the heart brittle delicate easily shatters

desperate

it beats against the window. can't let it in
it eats and leaves no bone

no history/memory of having been

★

white birds do not eat them

9

in my soul winged beings flutter

dead/transformed
my mouth open. moths take flight

155

the ISM

tired i count the ways in which it determines my life
permeates everything. it's in the air
lives next door to me in stares of neighbors
meets me each day in the office. its music comes out the radio
drives beside me in my car. strolls along with me
down supermarket aisles
it's on television
and in the streets even when my walk is casual/undefined
it's overhead flashing lights
i find it in my mouth
when i would speak of other things

THE BIG EMPTY

—*for Kalin*

high. i am lost. it finds. me.
appears. i stare at it as it
mushrooms. fills my eyes
long long into nothing/void
billows/night clouds
an endless dishwater grey ocean
consumes/consumed
my mouth throat fill with it
no light no light no light
first silence. then soft drum/heart beat
loud. louder. breaks my ear
what i must do i can't do/slay
it lays on me in me

*

can't cry it away can't talk it away can't
fight it away can't
eye upon me i scream in its sun/sear
tear me from this cross
end my pain
wash it away in blood
take this towel/my life
throw it in

the head of my baby
spills open/an egg
words cum
running out

SHOPPING BAG LADY

she winds her way down dark dingy avenues/alleys/mind
picks over discarded years looking for a good one
scavenging heartaches, pain, fear, disappointment
sparse nourishment for her toothless ever sucking mouth
rags, tatters and bits of courage to clothe
her fat lumpy black form or make patches or rejuvenate
for re-sale to some denizen of salvage
she keeps an eager eye out for love/rare as a lost diamond pendant
she rears and gags when the stench of hatred overcomes
leans against graffiti'd walls till nausea subsides
or cackles joy over the half emptied contents of romance/
a vintage wine tickles her ancient tongue
she seeks lost items for meager profit
swears rackish when she finds nothing
gloats and hums her way to the bus stop when
booty is plentiful and prospects for an evening meal improved

THE SATURDAY AFTERNOON BLUES

can kill you
can fade your life away
friends are all out shopping
ain't nobody home
suicide hotline is busy
and here i am on my own
with a pill and a bottle for company
and heart full of been done wrong
i'm a candidate for the coroner, a lyric for a song

saturday afternoons are killers
when the air is brisk and warm
ol' sun he steady whispers
soon the life you know will be done
suicide line i can't get you
best friend out of town
alone with a pill and a bottle
i drink my troubles down

the man i love is a killer
the man i love is a thief
the man i love is a junky
the man i love is grief

some call saturday the sabbath
it's the bottom of the line some say
whether last or first, my heart's gonna burst
and there ain't no help my way
here with a pill and a bottle
and a life full of been done wrong
i'm a candidate for the coroner, a lyric
for a song

I ARRIVE HOME TO THE FUNERAL

still brown boxes greet me
all that's left
no ashes no bone
as if he disappeared into thin air

couldn't get the marriage certificate off the wall
as tho held there by magnet force
instead of one flat tack

last night my son dreamt of madness and the
bloody butchered body of a child
he never wants to dream that dream again

yes devils yes gods now i will believe in anything

the skeleton disrobes
removes each layer of skin
strips away muscle and vein
casts off the mannered meat
beds down in the coffin/truth

you must understand
i didn't go looking for it
it found me

THE CHILDREN

are out in the world now. on their own
people hear them and see them and say
are you sure they're yours? they don't look like you
and i smile. every now and then one
hits home for a visit and brings tears or joy
and when they do things i don't like
there's nothing i can effectively say or do
they have their own lives now
and no matter how good they are or bad
they are mine
mama will never deny them
once in print

HISTORY

today god is not home
she is out seducing beggars

she turns his wine sour
makes his seed sterile
withers his hope

harridan

there is no desire in me to combat the years. i look forward

this bird her wings spread
rises from the ash of his flesh

"what you need is a sugar daddy"

sweet his flesh is sweet as california october air
sweet his touch as sweet as the first spoon of ice cream
sweet his fuck sweet as plum wine

last night he came for money
a dinner of pork and rice
the baby's smile
a few hours of television
to be part of this life for a moment
and after he took me
quick against the floor

so there will be a job maybe
and the psych wants to talk to him again
and i keep wondering about all the
shit making it impossible: living
black to black

"it's better," the gypsy said
"with this guy cuz he's got the same kind of skin i've got"

tomorrow i may escape the box
fanfare will sound
the top pop open
i will leap into space and never come down

I LOVE THE DARK

—*for Eloise Klein Healy*

it is its own idea
like breath
it knows. does not have to be told

the dark is omni
(his hand on my breast. my skin sees)
a voice calls
my name vacant avenue motel blue a lone walker

the dark cocoon at the beginning of my life

storm in his eyes my lover hurt
rainy winter days. hot chocolate and
devil's food cake
it's hide-and-seek i'm safe in its cloak
can't be found or lay in the bed of it eyes open
hungry for his touch

early eve. i wait. dark arrives/grape crush velvet
curtain falls. an old friend
we smile. reminisce
i sense it warm a throb between my thighs
movement. slow. easy. sensual

smell of fresh wet black earth

out of the dark
a phone rings his erotic need
it fills the space called bedroom
gives birth to obeah/Vudu/jazz
is for escapists to dress in

i move thru dark
waters quell, free my imagination
i hear sunset/a lone sax wail/pulse
compels, tremors

night wakes

i welcome you dark
soft. gentle. my mother's hands

DEATH 424

.

night's voyage/his eyes my dream
our kiss circular rhythms of tongues
and teeth in passion's dance
express a kindred hunger
in his wake
cold lonely dawn and damp sheets
it's the year of cocaine and coors
crazed blond men and confused black men
hear the bay of the she-hound gone mad
casting off her domesticity, running with wolves
and that moon
oh ugly eye of ash moon

I'VE WRITTEN THIS POEM BEFORE

in blood my blood
staining drapes, the divan, the print of "pimp tempts woman to
    whore"
i've penned it tossing restless in cold sheets in
early AMs
scrawled it while stalled in eternal lines of welfare recipients
awaiting word
scratched it line by pained line
into creases of county jail mattresses damp with sweat and hope
    for bail
recorded this verse a dozen times
with my eyes scouring endless avenues seeking for rent signs
children allowed
i've repeated my never spent agony
into countless ears of too fucking understanding many who
    misunderstood
so i'm writing it again
one more time in black and white with hope that
someone out there will at last
get it straight

I AM EVERYTHING

look. this flesh/cosmos/divinity
into this realm/earth/thought
        (his flesh tastes of my flesh our joining/struggle
        in night's embrace in his eye my smile rises)
horribly sane
black skin black bone black love
beauty articulate dangerous

the father and the mother

Printed July 1983 in Santa Barbara & Ann Arbor
for the Black Sparrow Press by Graham Mackintosh
& Edwards Brothers Inc. Design by Barbara Martin.
This edition is published in paper wrappers; there
are 200 hardcover trade copies; 200 hardcover copies
have been numbered & signed by the author; & 26
copies handbound in boards by Earle Gray are lettered
& signed by the author.

Photo: Michael J. Elderman

Wanda Coleman is a free-lance writer from Los Angeles. Now in her 30s, she has worked a variety of jobs and professions including medical filing clerk/transcriber, typist, script writer, editor of a national magazine and waitress. She received a literary fellowship from the National Endowment for the Arts 1981–82 and presently co-hosts "The Poetry Connexion," an interview program with Austin Straus for Los Angeles' Pacifica radio station. *Imagoes* is her second book of poetry.